Toward Deeper Reductions in U.S. and Russian Nuclear Weapons

COUNCIL *on*
FOREIGN
RELATIONS

Center for Preventive Action

Council Special Report No. 57
November 2010

Micah Zenko

Toward Deeper Reductions in U.S. and Russian Nuclear Weapons

The Council on Foreign Relations (CFR) is an independent, nonpartisan membership organization, think tank, and publisher dedicated to being a resource for its members, government officials, business executives, journalists, educators and students, civic and religious leaders, and other interested citizens in order to help them better understand the world and the foreign policy choices facing the United States and other countries. Founded in 1921, CFR carries out its mission by maintaining a diverse membership, with special programs to promote interest and develop expertise in the next generation of foreign policy leaders; convening meetings at its headquarters in New York and in Washington, DC, and other cities where senior government officials, members of Congress, global leaders, and prominent thinkers come together with Council members to discuss and debate major international issues; supporting a Studies Program that fosters independent research, enabling CFR scholars to produce articles, reports, and books and hold roundtables that analyze foreign policy issues and make concrete policy recommendations; publishing *Foreign Affairs*, the preeminent journal on international affairs and U.S. foreign policy; sponsoring Independent Task Forces that produce reports with both findings and policy prescriptions on the most important foreign policy topics; and providing up-to-date information and analysis about world events and American foreign policy on its website, CFR.org.

The Council on Foreign Relations takes no institutional positions on policy issues and has no affiliation with the U.S. government. All statements of fact and expressions of opinion contained in its publications are the sole responsibility of the author or authors.

Council Special Reports (CSRs) are concise policy briefs, produced to provide a rapid response to a developing crisis or contribute to the public's understanding of current policy dilemmas. CSRs are written by individual authors—who may be CFR fellows or acknowledged experts from outside the institution—in consultation with an advisory committee, and are intended to take sixty days from inception to publication. The committee serves as a sounding board and provides feedback on a draft report. It usually meets twice—once before a draft is written and once again when there is a draft for review; however, advisory committee members, unlike Task Force members, are not asked to sign off on the report or to otherwise endorse it. Once published, CSRs are posted on www.cfr.org.

For further information about CFR or this Special Report, please write to the Council on Foreign Relations, 58 East 68th Street, New York, NY 10065, or call the Communications office at 212.434.9888. Visit our website, CFR.org.

To submit a letter in response to a Council Special Report for publication on our website, CFR.org, you may send an email to CSReditor@cfr.org. Alternatively, letters may be mailed to us at: Publications Department, Council on Foreign Relations, 58 East 68th Street, New York, NY 10065. Letters should include the writer's name, postal address, and daytime phone number. Letters may be edited for length and clarity, and may be published online. Please do not send attachments. All letters become the property of the Council on Foreign Relations and will not be returned. We regret that, owing to the volume of correspondence, we cannot respond to every letter.

This report is printed on paper that is certified by SmartWood to the standards of the Forest Stewardship Council, which promotes environmentally responsible, socially beneficial, and economically viable management of the world's forests.

Mixed Sources
Product group from well-managed
forests and other controlled sources
www.fsc.org Cert no. SW-COC-001530
© 1996 Forest Stewardship Council

Contents

Foreword

The New START Treaty, signed by presidents Barack Obama and Dmitry Medvedev in April 2010, was an important achievement. It committed both countries to substantial reductions in their nuclear arsenals. Both countries are now limited to 1,550 deployed strategic nuclear warheads—far below the Cold War peak of 31,000 in the United States alone. Moreover, the treaty is just one of several recent examples of U.S.-Russia collaboration on nuclear issues. In just the past two years, the former adversaries also finalized an agreement on plutonium disposal and imposed UN sanctions against Iran in reaction to its nuclear program.

Despite these signs of progress, it is unwise to be complacent. Even after the implementation of the New START Treaty, the United States and Russia will command enough nuclear weapons to annihilate each other several times over. In this Council Special Report, Fellow for Conflict Prevention Micah Zenko argues that reducing nuclear weapons stockpiles even further—to one thousand warheads—would be both strategically and politically advantageous. It would decrease the risk of nuclear weapons theft and nuclear attack and increase international political support for future U.S. initiatives to reduce or control nuclear warheads, all while maintaining a credible nuclear deterrent.

To achieve such a significant reduction, the United States and Russia would need to reach agreement on three long-standing and contentious issues. Tactical nuclear weapons deployments will be the most difficult of these challenges, Zenko writes, since Russia has a much larger arsenal of these weapons than does the United States and will therefore take the brunt of the cuts. Missile defense is the second obstacle toward further significant nuclear reductions. Much work remains to secure Moscow's cooperation on—or acceptance of—the project. Finally, the United States and Russia must reach a verifiable agreement on the use of nuclear vehicles for conventional weapons delivery. It is difficult to overstate the potential danger if either country mistook a conventional missile for a nuclear one.

Toward Deeper Reductions in U.S. and Russian Nuclear Weapons makes a thoughtful contribution to the discussion on how to build a stable future with far fewer nuclear weapons. As the Senate begins its consideration of the New START Treaty, this CSR serves as a reminder that there is more work to be done.

Richard N. Haass
President
Council on Foreign Relations
November 2010

Acknowledgments

I would like to express my gratitude to the many people who made this report possible. To begin, thank you to CFR President Richard N. Haass and Director of Studies James M. Lindsay for providing me the opportunity to author this report, and for their insightful feedback along the way.

The report's advisory committee was an invaluable resource and made the report better at every stage. In particular, I am grateful to advisory committee members who went above the call of duty—namely, Steven K. Pifer, Pavel Podvig, Matthew Henry Kroenig, and Robert Gard. I owe a huge debt of gratitude to Linton Brooks, who chaired the advisory committee and provided comments on multiple drafts.

The report benefited from interviews with more than two dozen civilian and military officials and staff at the State Department, Pentagon, and National Security Council, as well as conversations with outside experts, particularly Alexi Arbatov, Dmitri Trenin, Brian Finlay, and Dinshaw Mistry.

I am also grateful to Patricia Dorff and Lia Norton in Publications for terrific editing support, and Lisa Shields, Anya Schmemann, and Melinda Brouwer in Communications and Marketing for marketing efforts. I appreciate the contributions of the Studies staff, including Andrew Lim and Amy Baker, in shepherding the report from start to finish.

Huge thanks are owed to the Center for Preventive Action (CPA) and the New York team in particular. I am very grateful for the logistical and research support of CPA intern Amy Cunningham, and especially appreciative of the repeated editing and improvements by Research Associate Rebecca R. Friedman. My colleague in Washington, CPA director Paul B. Stares, also offered valuable guidance and insights.

Finally, I am thankful for the edits and comments offered by my brother, Adam Zenko.

This work was made possible by a generous grant from the Plough-shares Fund. The statements made and views expressed herein are solely my own.

Micah Zenko

Council Special Report

Introduction

President Barack Obama has made reductions in the United States' nuclear arsenal and a decreased reliance on nuclear weapons major foreign policy priorities for his administration. The New Strategic Arms Reduction Treaty (New START), signed in April 2010 by President Obama and Russia's president, Dmitry Medvedev, represents concrete movement toward these goals—goals that both presidents share. This follow-on accord to the 1991 START Treaty limits the United States and Russia to 1,550 deployed strategic nuclear and conventional warheads, 800 strategic launchers, and 700 deployed strategic missiles and bombers. Yet while the New START Treaty represents a substantial decrease from Cold War levels, the United States will retain around 2,000 deployed strategic and tactical nuclear weapons and Russia will maintain approximately 3,500 deployed strategic and tactical nuclear weapons—which together will constitute over 90 percent of the world's nuclear weapons.

To achieve additional nuclear weapons reductions, the United States and Russia should pursue deeper cuts through a verifiable and legally binding bilateral treaty limiting each country to no more than one thousand operationally deployed nuclear weapons, including tactical nuclear weapons, which Washington and Moscow have not formally addressed since the 1987 Intermediate-Range Nuclear Forces Treaty.[1] By counting both strategic and tactical nuclear weapons, which no prior U.S.-Russia arms control agreement has done, this treaty would open a new chapter of arms control negotiations. Moreover, the overall reductions it would require surpass New START's 30 percent decrease from the warhead limit in the 2002 Strategic Offensive Reductions Treaty (SORT), which had a ceiling of 2,200 deployed strategic warheads. Hence, capping both countries' arsenals at one thousand deployed weapons would cut the United States' deployed arsenal in half and reduce Russia's by more than two-thirds.

A bilateral treaty between the United States and Russia would serve U.S. national interests in a number of ways:

- It would allow the United States to fulfill its security commitments by maintaining a credible nuclear deterrent that extends to allies and partners via the "nuclear triad" of land-, sea-, and air-based delivery vehicles.
- It would provide the current or future administrations political leverage and flexibility to seek additional verifiable reductions with Russia and initiate a series of multilateral agreements that include the participation of other nuclear weapon states.
- Deeper cuts in U.S. and Russian nuclear forces would help catalyze broader international support for a range of American nuclear priorities, such as securing all nuclear weapons materials within four years.
- Fewer operational tactical nuclear weapons deployed by the United States and Russia would decrease the likelihood of nuclear terrorism by reducing the total number of such weapons potentially vulnerable to diversion or theft.
- The treaty would also reduce the probability and severity of nuclear attack on the United States and its allies by diminishing the number of nuclear weapons that could target the United States and decreasing the perceived threat from Russian tactical nuclear weapons to U.S. allies.
- The successful negotiation and ratification of an additional bilateral nuclear reduction treaty would reinforce a "reset" of U.S.-Russia relations, which increases the likelihood of Moscow's cooperation on a broader set of critical U.S. foreign policy priorities.

Future U.S.-Russia nuclear reduction talks, however, face significant challenges. To create the conditions for an agreement, three substantive policy and technical issues must be addressed: tactical nuclear weapons, missile defense, and conventional weapons on nuclear-capable delivery systems. This report assesses these interrelated challenges and offers practical recommendations for surmounting them. It does not detail the specific provisions for a bilateral treaty, such as the types of permitted warheads, delivery vehicles, or inactive stockpiles.

Moving Toward One Thousand

For the reasons enumerated, the United States should pursue the deepest nuclear reductions possible while maintaining deterrence and political feasibility. A bilateral treaty limiting the United States and Russia to one thousand operationally deployed nuclear weapons achieves both objectives. (In this report, *weapons* and *warheads* are used interchangeably.)[2] An arsenal of one thousand nuclear weapons is more than sufficient to allow the U.S. military to sustain the nuclear triad to deter any plausible current and future threats, or respond with a devastating retaliation in the case of a nuclear first strike. During the Cold War, experts estimated that that the United States would need no more than five hundred weapons to fight a nuclear war against the Soviet Union.[3] While this scenario is highly implausible today, one thousand weapons would ensure that the United States could devastate any potential adversary in a nuclear exchange. Reducing the U.S. nuclear arsenal does not threaten American security because, unlike during the Cold War, when the U.S. nuclear arsenal compensated for conventional shortcomings vis-à-vis the Soviet Union, today the United States retains an overwhelming edge in conventional power-projection capabilities. Moreover, because the treaty would not count inactive stockpiles, it would allow the United States to rapidly build up its operationally deployed nuclear forces should Russia withdraw from extant arms control agreements or China increase its nuclear capabilities to a threatening level. Reducing the U.S. arsenal to one thousand is thus a cautious next step that diminishes the world's largest nuclear stockpiles while preserving strategic stability.

Consequently, both nuclear disarmament advocates and proponents of the continued primacy of nuclear weapons are likely to agree that moving to one thousand serves U.S. national interests. The former will view this treaty as a moderate and necessary bridge for later verifiable reductions by the United States and Russia, as well as a multilateral agreement that requires the participation of other declared nuclear weapons states; the latter will view the treaty as a strategic move that enhances American security without sacrificing U.S. deterrent capabilities. Conceivably such broad consensus would translate into bipartisan support from civilian and military officials. Indeed, several senior U.S. and Russian officials have already promoted a move toward one thousand, indicating comfort with this number among decision-makers.[4] The treaty would also balance the positions of allied governments who favor faster movement toward nuclear disarmament against those who maintain that robust U.S. nuclear capabilities are necessary.

Given the size of U.S. and Russian arsenals, Moscow is the only appropriate partner in the move toward one thousand. China, with an estimated 240 nuclear weapons, should not be included in this round of cuts; future negotiations must include Beijing, however.[5] Unlike other nuclear weapons powers with arsenals in the mid-hundreds (France and the United Kingdom), China is the only other potentially threatening nuclear power—a strategic competitor of both Russia and the United States—whose nuclear and conventional capabilities are quantitatively and qualitatively improving.[6] While China is currently unwilling to consider any substantive discussions on nuclear weapons issues, Washington and Moscow should initiate a parallel nuclear dialogue with Beijing that lays the foundation for a future trilateral arms control treaty.[7] Such an agreement must place a ceiling on China's arsenal to prevent it from launching an arms race as the United States and Russia reduce their nuclear weapons stockpiles to the lowest levels since the 1950s.

Nuclear Forces After
the New START Treaty

Within seven years after the New START Treaty goes into effect, the United States and Russia must reduce their arsenals to 1,550 deployed nuclear warheads and 700 deployed strategic missiles and bombers. For the United States, these strategic missiles and bombers—defined as long-range delivery vehicles with high-yield weapons—constitute the nuclear triad of long-range bombers, intercontinental ballistic missiles, and nuclear submarines it plans to sustain for the foreseeable future to mitigate unexpected technological failure or geopolitical surprise that could render one leg of the triad vulnerable.[8] Along with its deployed strategic arsenal, the United States will retain an inactive stockpile of some one to two thousand warheads. The New START Treaty does not include limits on nonstrategic—or tactical—nuclear weapons, and the United States will likely retain tactical arsenals comparable to those today. While Washington and Moscow have yet to agree on a common, technical definition of tactical nuclear weapons, they generally have lower yields, are intended for shorter ranges, and are designed for battlefield use. The United States reportedly has four hundred operationally deployed tactical nuclear weapons and another seven hundred in inactive reserve.[9] U.S. operational tactical nuclear weapons are maintained at the Seymour Johnson Air Force Base in North Carolina, and at bases in five North Atlantic Treaty Organization (NATO) countries, with inactive reserves at bases in Nevada and New Mexico.[10]

It is considerably more difficult to assess the current and future state of Russian nuclear forces. After New START, Russia's arsenal will reportedly contain a strategic nuclear triad comparable to today and an inactive stockpile of several thousand warheads.[11] Currently, Russia's tactical nuclear arsenal is estimated to contain two thousand operationally deployed tactical nuclear weapons—some of which may be dedicated to a missile defense system for Moscow—and some thirty-four hundred in inactive reserve.[12] Russia keeps most of its operationally deployed tactical weapons at nuclear-certified bases near NATO's borders, and its inactive reserves at permanent storage sites in central Russia.[13] Tactical nuclear weapons at Russia's nuclear-certified bases are believed to be more vulnerable to diversion or theft than those at permanent storage sites.[14] Like the United States, Russia is unlikely to substantially diminish its nonstrategic arsenal absent a negotiated agreement requiring reductions.

Tactical Nuclear Weapons

The most difficult issue that the United States and Russia must address before negotiating deeper nuclear reductions is each country's nonstrategic—or tactical—nuclear weapons. In 1991, presidents George H.W. Bush and Mikhail Gorbachev announced the unilateral and nonbinding Presidential Nuclear Initiatives, which eliminated a range of tactical nuclear weapons and withdrew others from operational deployment for dismantlement or consolidation at permanent nuclear storage sites. This initiative was reaffirmed the following year by presidents Bush and Boris Yeltsin. Later attempts in the 1990s to discuss tactical weapons failed, largely due to resistance from Russia's armed forces. Nevertheless, for a bilateral treaty that limits both countries to one thousand operationally deployed nuclear weapons, most reductions—especially for Russia—will come from tactical weapons. Since Russia maintains a significantly larger tactical arsenal—and places great importance on it for territorial defense—unprecedented transparency and cuts will require greater sacrifices from Moscow.

The primary use of U.S. tactical nuclear weapons is reinforcement of the nuclear umbrella that extends to at least thirty-one allied countries—the twenty-seven other members of NATO, Japan, South Korea, Australia, and possibly Taiwan—as well as other "partner" countries that do not have mutual defense treaties with the United States. NATO benefits from tactical nuclear deterrence through an arrangement whereby U.S. B-61 tactical nuclear warheads are forward-deployed in Europe under American military custody but are on hand for delivery by European or U.S. dual-capable aircraft.[15] As a practical matter, B-61s are a political symbol of America's commitment to defending Europe; as one Pentagon official acknowledged, "There are no war plans in NATO for using [the B-61s]."[16] These warheads are believed to be maintained at air bases in Belgium, Germany, Italy, the Netherlands, and Turkey.[17] Similarly, the United States provides tactical nuclear deterrence to allies and partners in Asia through tactical nuclear weapons that can be deployed in times of crisis through forward-deploying heavy bombers or dual-capable aircraft to the region. Removing some B-61s from Europe, or having fewer operational tactical nuclear weapons that can be deployed to Asia, would require a credible and adequate substitution of strategic nuclear capabilities, missile defenses, or conventional military power.

Confusion remains about the role and mission of Russia's tactical nuclear arsenal. Many U.S. officials claim that Russia has expanded the potential uses of its tactical arsenal, though this is not apparent from recent official statements or military doctrine.[18] Russia's (unclassified) military doctrine calls for the use of nuclear weapons in response to an attack involving nuclear or weapons of mass destruction (WMD) against Russia or its allies and "in the event of aggression against the Russian Federation involving the use of conventional weapons when the very existence of the state is under threat."[19] This latter option is intended for deterring NATO's vastly superior conventional military power.

Two conditions must be met for Russia to agree to tactical nuclear weapons talks: the first is to negotiate the removal of U.S. tactical nuclear weapons from Europe, which threaten Russia's conventional and nuclear forces; the second is to meet the Russian demand to reopen multilateral discussions on the stalled Adapted Treaty on Conventional Armed Forces in Europe (CFE Treaty), from which Russia suspended its participation in 2007. An updated CFE Treaty would mitigate NATO's conventional predominance in Europe by further reducing offensive conventional weapons systems within an inspection regime that allays Russia's European security concerns. In summer 2010, U.S. officials proposed three basic principles to guide future CFE Treaty discussions: maximum transparency for reporting force levels, military exercises, and military infrastructure plans; reciprocal restraints on conventional forces in the northern and southern "flank" regions; and host nation consent for the stationing of troops and equipment. Administration officials hope to reach consensus on these principles with their Russian counterparts in time for a joint announcement by presidents Obama and Medvedev in late 2010. While the principles are intended to inform an updated agreement—dubbed CFE Three—Obama administration officials insist that NATO conventional military levels should not be conditional on operational tactical nuclear weapons cuts.[20]

Some Russian analysts, however, claim that the military threat from China is inevitably growing more significant as Beijing enhances its conventional power projection and nuclear capabilities.[21] Military improvements, combined with the sheer size of territory potentially vulnerable to Chinese aggression, have led some experts to suggest that Russia should retain its tactical arsenal as a hedge against future threats from the Far East.[22] However, neither Russia's national security strategy nor its military doctrine mentions or even implies a threat from China, enhancing possible misunderstandings about what its tactical nuclear weapons are intended to do.

The broad outlines of an agreement on tactical nuclear weapons are already apparent: reciprocal data exchange of the size, location, and related delivery system of the relevant weapons; verification procedures to enforce the provisions of the treaty; and an accepted categorization for the class of weapons systems to be included and their operational status.[23] Given earlier failed attempts at bilateral talks on tactical nuclear weapons, it will be difficult—though necessary—for both Washington and Moscow to take the unprecedented steps required on these three issues.

First, each country should reveal its tactical nuclear weapons inventory, location, and operational status, either publicly or through a private data exchange mechanism, to produce a comprehensive database. To assuage Russia's concerns about the security of its declared tactical arsenal, there are well-established information technologies that "allow states to exchange detailed stockpile data while maintaining complete control over access to its contents."[24]

The second component of an agreement on tactical nuclear weapons reductions is a verification of any data exchanged and a confirmation that the provisions of the treaty have been implemented on an agreed timeline. While verifying limits on Russia's operational tactical nuclear arsenal would be challenging, U.S. officials believe that if the Kremlin reverses its earlier opposition, there are sufficient verification procedures and techniques available to ensure Russian compliance with any treaty provisions.[25] In the past fifteen years, there has been an increase in the number and scope of demonstrated technologies and procedures that could provide adequate verification, including the use of radiation detection, remote measurement, and tamper-indicating tags.[26]

Finally, two important categorization issues require clarification. There is no universally accepted categorization of tactical nuclear weapons. However, the United States and Russia have published definitions sufficiently similar that they could be combined for the purposes of a bilateral treaty.[27] In addition to short-range tactical bombs, all nuclear weapons not designed for use on intercontinental ballistic missiles (ICBMs), submarine launched ballistic missiles (SLBMs), and heavy bombers should fall under any joint U.S.-Russia definition.

The more important categorization issue is what should constitute an "operationally deployed" tactical nuclear weapon. Unlike strategic nuclear weapons, which can be launched at short notice, tactical weapons are not routinely loaded on U.S. or Russian delivery vehicles. In both countries, however, there are distinctions between military bases certified for maintaining operational and nonoperational tactical nuclear weapons. Operational storage sites contain tactical nuclear weapons equipped for deployment on short notice, as well as air or naval delivery systems; permanent, or nonoperational, storage sites contain warheads rendered unusable due to removal of tritium and other critical components, and these sites do not house delivery vehicles. The United States and Russia each clearly understand the distinction between these sites.[28]

The goal of tactical nuclear weapons limitation talks would be to agree to a list of bases where any tactical nuclear weapons would be considered operational, and permanent storage sites where they would be monitored as inactive reserves. Russia and the United States could employ the range of verification procedures used extensively and effectively for the START I Treaty to monitor operational and permanent storage sites. These methods ensure a high degree of confidence that cheating would be detected promptly and decisively.[29] To make tactical nuclear weapons limitations permanent, both sides should verifiably dismantle nonoperational warheads at assembly-disassembly facilities at the Pantex Plant in the United States and either the Trekhgorny, Zlatoust-36, or Lesnoy, Sverdlovsk-45, sites in Russia. Dismantling thousands of warheads will take decades; the current projected dismantlement queue in the United States stretches to 2022. In the interim, inactive tactical nuclear stockpiles will provide a technical and geopolitical hedge should either country shirk its arms control commitments—though refurbishing large numbers of nonoperational weapons for use would require time, and their redeployment to nuclear-capable bases would be detected.

Missile Threats and Missile Defenses

To protect U.S. allies, partners, and civilian and military personnel deployed abroad from states like Iran and North Korea, the George W. Bush and Obama administrations both proposed ballistic missile defense (BMD) strategies for Europe. Though each strategy intended to take Russian political and military concerns into account, both encountered strong resistance from Russian officials. Since U.S. missile defense capabilities in Europe will quantitatively and qualitatively improve as the number of Russian ICBMs decreases, it will be necessary to provide additional assurances to Moscow of the intentions and capabilities of missile defense in a bilateral treaty that limits each country to one thousand operationally deployed nuclear weapons. This will require going further than the New START Treaty, which does not place any constraints on U.S. missile defense programs or deployment plans.

In September 2009, the Obama administration canceled its predecessor's European missile defense architecture, claiming that an updated National Intelligence Estimate (NIE) found that Iran was producing and deploying short- and medium-range missiles faster than previously projected, and that there were steady improvements in missile defense sensor and interceptor capabilities for tracking and engaging them. Undoubtedly, the intention to reset U.S.-Russia relations played a role, though administration officials denied this was a direct consideration. President Medvedev hailed the decision and Russian military officials downplayed earlier threats against Europe, such as restationing short-range missiles in the Russian territory of Kaliningrad, which borders Poland and Lithuania.[30]

The Obama administration's Phased Adaptive Approach (PAA) ballistic missile defense strategy for Europe is a ten-year plan whereby U.S. interceptors will be deployed in four stages based on missile threat trend lines from Iran or other adversaries. Like other missile defense schemes, this ambitious strategy—particularly in the later stages—is based on a belief that unproven military capabilities can be supported and funded by Congress, demonstrated through realistic testing, and deployed on time. Administration officials have emphasized that if the timelines for effective radars or interceptors shift, or missile threats change, the PAA is "flexible," "scalable," and "rapidly re-locatable." These terms serve as placeholders as the Pentagon studies the appropriate mix of capabilities required, while also enhancing Russia's uncertainty about the system's eventual composition. The current PAA plan adheres to the following timeline.[31]

– 2011: Deploying two to three Aegis BMD ships, fielding between 80 to 120 Standard Missile-3 (SM-3) IA interceptors on twenty-four-hour patrols to the Mediterranean Sea and North Sea to attempt to cover southern Europe.

– 2015: Placing twenty-four land-based (still untested) SM-3 IB interceptors—or Aegis Ashore—in Romania to triple the amount of territory under protection.

– 2018: Placing twenty-four faster land-based (undeveloped) SM-3 IIA interceptors in Poland to protect the entire land mass of Europe.

– 2020: Upgrading both land-based sites with the faster and more capable (undeveloped) SM-3 IIB interceptors that could intercept Iranian ICBMs threatening Europe and the United States.

The bottom-line Russian interest in U.S. missile defenses is to ensure that they do not develop "quantitatively or qualitatively in such a way that threatens the potential of Russia's strategic nuclear forces."[32] This objective is consistent with stated U.S. missile defense policy.[33] Russian officials recognize that the first two stages of the PAA system cannot pose such a threat, since the velocity of SM-3 Block IA/IB interceptors based at sea—or in Romania and Poland—would not endanger Russia's land-based ICBMs flying over the Arctic, or its Northern and Pacific Fleet submarine forces in their home ports. However, some Russian experts are concerned that the performance characteristics of the SM-3 IIA and IIBs, scheduled for deployment in 2018 and 2020, could threaten Russia's ICBM force.[34] Russian misperceptions are understandable given the outstanding questions that remain about the eventual PAA architecture. How many Aegis BMD ships will be on station in Europe?

Will such ships be routinely deployed to the Norwegian Sea or Barents Sea? Will the SM-3 IIB be liquid-fueled, and therefore less compatible with Aegis ships? How many land-based SM-3 IIBs will eventually be placed in Romania and Poland?[35] According to U.S. officials, no Standard interceptor missiles will have the velocity or range to catch up to much faster Russian ICBMs.[36]

To alleviate Russian concerns, the Obama administration is pursuing joint missile defense, much as previous administrations unsuccessfully attempted in the 1990s. Such unprecedented collaboration could be a transformative opportunity for U.S.-Russia relations, but the Obama administration will need to weigh Russia's desire to be a meaningful participant against Congress's demand for robust missile defense.

The Obama administration hopes that Russia will participate in the PAA system with its own radar and sensory systems, thereby recognizing that missile defenses do not threaten its strategic nuclear force. The most immediate form of cooperation that has been discussed in bilateral working groups is integrating Russia's existing high-frequency early-warning radars in Armavir, Russia, and Gabala, Azerbaijan, into Europe's missile defense architecture. These radars, though well situated for acquiring and tracking missiles launched from Iran, are not useful for assisting the Standard interceptors from discriminating among decoys and engaging missiles in mid-course. As a Pentagon official noted of Russia's early-warning radars, "The technology isn't great, but the geography is perfect."[37] One option is to upgrade the radars to support the Standard in fire control and missile engagement. Such cooperation, however, might aggravate Russian fears, as Pentagon officials have indicated that any Russian participation in the PAA would only be to supplement American sensors and missiles. Currently, there is no conceivable joint structure whereby Russia could hold a veto over the launch of a Standard missile to attempt to intercept a ballistic missile from Iran or elsewhere.

Joint threat assessment remains a significant stumbling block to robust U.S.-Russia missile defense collaboration. The explicit focus of the European PAA missile defense system is to counter Iran's potential nuclear weapon and ballistic missile threats, a subject on which U.S. and Russian officials hold divergent views. In March, Russian foreign minister Sergei Lavrov asserted that "Iran has no missiles capable of striking Europe . . . and is unlikely to develop [such missiles] in the foreseeable future."[38] Russia's ambassador to NATO, Dmitry Rogozin, went so far as to write that Iran could not create "within the next twenty years a ballistic missile capable of striking the territory of the U.S. or any of NATO's European allies."[39] Both projections are strikingly at odds with the findings of the 2009 NIE. Moreover, in addition to the skepticism of U.S. intelligence, many Russian officials believe that the United States simply exaggerates Iranian threats as a pretext to expand and anchor U.S. influence within the former Soviet sphere.

In an attempt to forge a closer consensus, the Obama administration has conducted a round of joint threat assessments of ballistic missile threats with U.S. and Russian government experts. The meetings have shown some promise, with Russian experts generally accepting that Iran has made recent and unexpected strides in its short-range and medium-range ballistic missile capabilities. Less certain is whether future joint threat assessments can reach a degree of consensus over the direction and scope of Iran's avowed ICBM goals.[40] Moreover, it remains to be seen whether an assessment of Iran's ballistic missile threats made by such joint expert working groups will be matched by future official Russian statements and lead to U.S.-Russia missile defense collaboration.

Conventional Weapons on Nuclear-Capable Delivery Systems

In the coming decades, hundreds of strategic delivery systems will remain in the force structure even as the U.S. nuclear arsenal shrinks. Given the costs already spent in developing and deploying them, some of these weapons systems will be provided with updated, nonnuclear roles and missions. They will increasingly be dedicated to conventional missions that administration officials acknowledge are a more relevant, usable, and responsive "series of graded options that can be a realistic, serious deterrent."[41] These nonnuclear strike capabilities will increasingly become an important though limited tool in U.S. military strategy to hold at risk distant, deeply buried, and time-sensitive targets that cannot be threatened by other nonnuclear means. To preserve the integrity of the arms control regime, these systems should be permitted but counted under the nuclear warhead ceilings.

Russian officials are most concerned about the concept of Prompt Global Strike (PGS), listed as the fourth greatest external military threat in Russian military doctrine.[42] While PGS has neither a common definition nor concept of operations, most Pentagon officials envision it as simply a niche capability that could be called upon to strengthen regional deterrence architectures. Others have a more expansive notion of potential missions, including providing the president with "near-nuclear" options.[43] Secretary of Defense Robert M. Gates has described PGS as the capability to "attack targets anywhere on the globe in an hour or less."[44] PGS programs have received enhanced research and development funding that was recently projected to grow from $70 million in FY2009 to $575 million for FY2015.[45]

Near-term potential PGS capabilities involve replacing nuclear warheads on U.S.-based Minuteman III ICBMs with conventional payloads (or no munition at all, thus relying on kinetic impact). The fielding date for this Conventional Strike Missile has slipped from 2015 to 2017, and now perhaps to 2020.[46] Another PGS option would require modifying the Trident-D5 SLBM to hold conventional pay-loads, although Congress cut funding for this Conventional Trident Modification program in 2008. Whether deployed on ICBMs or SLBMs, conventional PGS systems would count against the 1,550 strategic warhead limit in the New START Treaty. There are also pro-grams and budgets for more advanced and unproven PGS capabili-ties, such as the Falcon Hypersonic Technology Vehicle (HTV), which would fly through space carrying conventional bombs, reenter the atmosphere, and then glide on a maneuverable path for several thou-sand miles at hypersonic speeds to a target.[47] According to U.S. offi-cials, such "boost-glide" HTV systems would not count against New START Treaty limits.[48]

While operational PGS systems are five to ten years away, Rus-sian officials have already expressed several concerns. First, and most important, U.S. conventional missile launches from nuclear-capable delivery systems could be misinterpreted by Russia's reportedly unre-liable early-warning radar system as carrying a nuclear payload, thus potentially prompting an unintentional retaliatory nuclear strike. Second, PGS may blur the nuclear bright-line, as some PGS conven-tional weapons "have the capabilities similar to those of smaller nuclear warheads," according to General Vladimir Verkhovtsev, chief of the 12th Main Directorate.[49] Indeed, this is an explicit goal of the system, with Vice Chairman of the Joint Chiefs of Staff General James E. Cartwright noting that "prompt global strike should also serve as an alternative to comparable nuclear weapons, particularly where the use of nuclear weapons would be inappropriate."[50] Third, some fear PGS systems could upset the strategic balance through conventional coun-terforce strikes against Russian military targets.

In response to nuclear ambiguity concerns, several solutions have been proposed that could distinguish the payload of conventional mis-sile launches from nuclear-capable systems. Some build on existing transparency mechanisms, whereas others are untested and novel for PGS-specific missions. All of these proposals have their shortcom-ings, which could be exacerbated during international crisis situations. Among the more politically and technically feasible proposals: declar-ing one ICBM field as being "conventional only" and allowing Rus-sian inspections to verify that missiles deployed there could not carry nuclear payloads; providing video monitoring of ICBM silos or SLBM tubes of missile shrouds containing conventional payloads; using a depressed trajectory for conventional strikes to distinguish them from nuclear ICBMs that follow a parabolic arc; designing a new missile with a distinct boost signature for conventional-only missions; and notifying Russia shortly before a PGS launch, through the Agreement on Notifications of ICBM and SLBM Launches or the currently moribund Joint Data Exchange Center.[51] As of June 2010, the Pentagon was still studying how to resolve the nuclear ambiguity concern for PGS systems.[52]

Russian strategic nuclear weapons can also be operationally deployed on a nuclear triad of land-, sea-, and air-based systems, each of which could also carry conventional warheads. However, Russia apparently has no concrete plans or programs to develop and deploy PGS-like capabilities. Given the constraints on its defense budget and competing priorities to modernize its nuclear capabilities, Russia probably will not attempt to match U.S. PGS programs.

Conclusion and Recommendations

Without resolution of the three interlinked issues described in this report, a bilateral treaty limiting the United States and Russia to one thousand operationally deployed nuclear weapons will be impossible. Specifically, four things must happen for such a treaty to be possible: New START Treaty ratification and preliminary implementation; agreement on an updated CFE Treaty; discussions between U.S. and Russian officials on controlling operational tactical nuclear weapons; and an understanding between the United States and Russia about U.S. missile defense capabilities that will not put a diminished arsenal of Russian ICBMs at risk, including possible missile defense collaboration.

Such progress toward deeper nuclear cuts will require sustained improvement in U.S.-Russia relations. Preliminarily, the Obama administration's "reset" has successfully produced Russian cooperation on nuclear priorities, such as finalizing a plutonium disposition agreement, negotiating the New START Treaty, and imposing additional United Nations sanctions against and canceling the transfer of advanced S300 surface-to-air missile systems to Iran. Going forward, bilateral relations must be strong enough to preserve nuclear arms control as an overriding strategic priority, immune to inevitable disagreements between Washington and Moscow over common approaches to other issues. As President Medvedev noted regarding nuclear reduction talks, "[the] negotiation process is not for the pleasure of the process itself, but it is done in order to reach practical, specific outcomes."[53] Closer and more enduring U.S.-Russia relations are especially important since—given that the New START Treaty required ninety meetings over the course of one year—those specific outcomes will not be reached until a second Obama term, or until after a forty-sixth president is elected.

   The following recommendations outline a framework for moving toward the next round of bilateral arms control negotiations.

*LIMITING OPERATIONAL
TACTICAL NUCLEAR WEAPONS*

– The Obama administration should use the Bilateral Presidential Commission Working Group on Arms Control and International Security to discuss practical and near-term confidence-building measures on tactical nuclear weapons with Russia.

– The Obama administration should reverse existing policy that prohibits funding enhanced security upgrades at all of Russia's frontline bases where tactical nuclear weapons are maintained with some level of operational status.

– Because Russia and NATO will revisit the stalled CFE Treaty, the Obama administration should reach consensus with NATO allies about what changes in allied conventional forces could be implemented to induce Russian cuts in operational tactical nuclear weapons.

– The Obama administration should direct the intelligence community to produce an updated assessment of Russia's inventory of tactical nuclear weapons, operational status, location, and supporting military doctrine.

U.S.-RUSSIA MISSILE DEFENSE COLLABORATION

– The Obama administration should continue joint ballistic missile threat assessments, system effectiveness assessments, exercises, and computer modeling and simulations with Russia. It should do so both bilaterally and through the NATO-Russia Council.

– Given Russian suspicions about the capabilities and intentions of missile defenses, the Bilateral Presidential Commission Working Group on Arms Control and International Security should provide Russian officials with regular briefings on the expected Phased Adaptive Approach architecture through 2020.

– As an early-warning mechanism for ballistic missile launches, the Obama administration should revive the Joint Data Exchange Center (JDEC), which has been needlessly delayed by Russia over tax and liability issues. The agreement is supposed to expire in 2010, but can be extended for five years if both countries agree.

- The Obama administration should promote Russian missile defense collaboration in the European PAA, at minimum through the integration of the early-warning radars in Armavir, Russia, and Gabala, Azerbaijan.

- The Pentagon plans to have thirty-eight Aegis BMD ships by 2015. Assuming the normal three-to-one rule of deployment-rest-reset, the United States could field more than a dozen Aegis ships at any time. The Obama administration should discuss with Russia how many ships it will normally deploy in support of the PAA in Europe, as opposed to other regions.

- Given Russian concerns about the European PAA capabilities scheduled for deployment by 2018 and 2020, Washington and Moscow should be seeking an agreement on U.S.-Russia missile defense collaboration well beforehand.

CONVENTIONAL WEAPONS ON NUCLEAR-CAPABLE DELIVERY SYSTEMS

- The Pentagon should develop a common definition and supporting doctrine for Prompt Global Strike to clarify the concept within the U.S. government, and provide transparency to allay Russian fears about potential capabilities and missions.[54]

- Although the administration maintains that boost-glide PGS capabilities would not be counted under New START, they should be counted in future treaties, since they have comparable military capabilities to nuclear-armed ballistic missiles, which are counted as strategic delivery vehicles. In preparation, the Pentagon should consider possible arms control constraints on boost-glide systems while it studies the appropriate mix of capabilities for PGS.[55]

- The administration should conduct a comprehensive analysis of all available technical mechanisms that could provide reliable transparency for conventional payloads mounted on strategic delivery vehicles.[56]

- The Obama administration should direct the intelligence community to conduct an assessment of what effects U.S. PGS capabilities would have on the global regime in restraining ballistic missile proliferation.

Endnotes

1. Operationally deployed nuclear weapons would include all warheads mated to delivery vehicles and in storage areas at nuclear-capable military bases.

2. Office of the Deputy Assistant to the Secretary of Defense (Nuclear Matters), *Nuclear Matters: A Practical Guide*, 2008, pp. 230, 235.

3. Ivo Daalder and Jan Lodal, "The Logic of Zero," *Foreign Affairs*, November/December 2008.

4. Interviews with State and Pentagon officials, March-June 2010; John Kerry, "New Directions for Foreign Relations," *Boston Globe*, January 13, 2009, p. A13; Ivo Daalder and Jan Lodal, "The Logic of Zero," *Foreign Affairs*, November/December 2008; "Russia Needs No Less Than 1,000 Strategic Nuke Warheads," *ITAR-TASS*, March 30, 2010; and Tim Reid, "President Obama Seeks Russia Deal to Slash Nuclear Weapons," *Times (London)*, February 4, 2009.

5. Robert Norris and Hans Kristensen, "Global Nuclear Weapon Inventories, 1945–2010," *Bulletin of the Atomic Scientists*, July/August 2010.

6. Office of the Secretary of Defense, *Annual Report to Congress: Military and Security Developments Involving the People's Republic of China 2010*, p. 34.

7. Interviews with State Department and Pentagon officials, April-June 2010.

8. According to Pentagon officials, retaining the triad was emphasized in the Nuclear Posture Review of 2010 to deal with scenarios where an adversary unexpectedly developed the capability to track U.S. nuclear-capable submarines. Interviews with Pentagon officials, April 2010.

9. This total includes the TLAM-N retirement. Norris and Kristensen, "U.S. Nuclear Forces, 2010," *Bulletin of the Atomic Scientists*, May/June 2010, p. 67.

10. Norris and Kristensen, "U.S. Nuclear Forces, 2010," pp. 67–68. This total includes the retirement of the TLAM-N from bases in Washington and Georgia.

11. Robert Norris and Hans Kristensen, "Russian Nuclear Forces, 2010," *Bulletin of the Atomic Scientists* January/February 2010, pp. 74–81; and Amy F. Woolf, "The New START Treaty: Central Limits and Key Provisions," Congressional Research Service, June 18, 2010, p. 20.

12. Norris and Kristensen, "Russian Nuclear Forces, 2010," p. 74.

13. Interview with State Department and Pentagon officials, March and April 2010; testimony of Secretary of State Hillary Clinton before the Senate Armed Services Committee, June 17, 2010. According to the Chief of the General Staff of the Russian Armed Forces, "there are no nuclear weapons in Kaliningrad." "Russian General Staff Chief Restates U.S. Missile Shield, NATO Expansion Concerns," *Interfax*, February 24, 2010.

14. As a matter of policy, the United States funded enhanced security upgrades for most permanent nuclear storage sites in Russia, but not for frontline nuclear-capable bases since it could enhance Russian military capability. Government Accountability Office,

Nuclear Nonproliferation: Progress Made in Improving Security at Russian Nuclear Sites, but the Long-term Sustainability of U.S.-Funded Security Upgrades Is Uncertain, February 2007, p. 20; interview with U.S. officials, May-June 2010; Matt Bunn, *Securing the Bomb 2010*, Project on Managing the Atom, Belfer Center for Science and International Affairs, Harvard University, March 2010, p. 96.

15. Robert Norris and Hans Kristensen, "Worldwide Deployments of Nuclear Weapons, 2009," *Bulletin of the Atomic Scientists*, November/December 2009, pp. 90–94. According to NATO, "In 2002, the readiness requirements for these [dual-capable] aircraft were further reduced and are now being measured in months." NATO, "NATO's Nuclear Forces in the New Security Environment," October 22, 2009.

16. Interview with Pentagon official, April 2010. For senior U.S. military officials who echo this sentiment, see Steve Pifer et al., *U.S. Nuclear and Extended Deterrence: Considerations and Challenges*, Brookings Institution Press, Arms Control Series, Paper 3, May 2010, p. 22.

17. Norris and Kristensen, "Nuclear Notebook: Worldwide Deployments of Nuclear Weapons, 2009," pp. 90–94.

18. Interview with State Department and Pentagon officials, March and April 2010.

19. Russian Federation, "The Military Doctrine of the Russian Federation," article XXII.

20. Interviews with State Department officials, May-June 2010.

21. Cristina Hansell and Nikita Perfilyev, "Together Toward Nuclear Zero: Understanding Chinese and Russian Security Concerns," *Nonproliferation Review*, November 2009, p. 444.

22. Miles Pomper, William Potter, and Nikolai Sokov, "Reducing Tactical Nuclear Weapons in Europe," *Survival*, February-March 2010, p. 77.

23. In addition to the arrangement discussed in this section, the Obama administration might trade permanent cuts in U.S. nondeployed strategic warheads for reductions in Russian tactical nuclear weapons.

24. National Academy of Sciences, *Monitoring Nuclear Weapons and Nuclear-Explosive Materials: An Assessment of Methods and Capabilities* (Washington, DC: National Academies Press, 2005), pp. 56–59.

25. Interviews with State Department and Pentagon officials, March and April 2010.

26. American Physical Society Panel on Public Affairs, *Technical Steps to Support Nuclear Arsenal Downsizing*, (Washington, DC: American Physical Society, February 2010), pp. 6–11.

27. See the comparable definitions in Joint Publication 1-02, *DOD Dictionary of Military and Associated Terms*, amended through April 2010, and NATO-Russia Council, NRC Nuclear Experts, *NATO-Russia Nuclear Glossary of Nuclear Terms and Definitions*, January 20, 2004, p. 1-23.

28. Interviews with U.S. officials, March-June 2010; interviews with Russian analysts, June 2010.

29. Interviews with Russian analysts, June 2010; Rose Gottemoeller, "Eliminating Short-Range Nuclear Weapons Designed to Be Forward Deployed," in George Schultz, Sidney Drell, and James Goodby, eds., *Reykjavik Revisited* (Stanford, CA: Hoover Institution, 2008), pp. 32–37; and Nikolai Sokov, "Strengthening the 1991 Declarations: Verification and Transparency Components," in Taino Susiluoto, ed., *Tactical Nuclear Weapons: Time for Control* (Geneva: United Nations Institute for Disarmament Research, 2002), pp. 93–132.

30. "Medvedev Praises Obama's Move on Europe Missile Shield," *RIA Novosti*, September 17, 2009; and "Russia Could Scrap Baltic Missile Plans Following U.S. Move," *RIA Novosti*, September 18, 2009.

31. DOD, Secretary of Defense Robert Gates and Vice Chairman of the Joint Chiefs of

Staff General James Cartwright press briefing, September 17, 2009; DOD, *Ballistic Missile Defense Review Report*, February 2010, pp. 24–32; hearing of the Senate Armed Services Committee, "Ballistic Missile Defense Policies," April 20, 2010; Deputy Assistant Secretary Frank A. Rose, Bureau of Verification, Compliance, and Implementation, "Challenges in Europe," remarks at the Sixth International Conference on Missile Defense, Lisbon, Portugal, February 10, 2010; and email communication with author from Missile Defense Agency, June 2010.

32. Kremlin, "Press Statement after Signing of Russia-US Treaty on Reduction and Limitation of Strategic Offensive Arms," April 8, 2010.

33. "Statement by the United States of America Concerning Missile Defense," April 7, 2010.

34. Sergey Rogov, "'Concepts': The 'Window of Opportunity' Is Open," *Nezavisimoye Voyennoye Obozreniye*, May 28, 2010; "NMD Breakthrough or Proliferation? Moskovskiy Komsomolets Experts Assess Changes to US Missile Defense in Europe," *Moskovskiy Komsomolets*, September 25, 2009, translation by World News Connection.

35. To achieve a faster velocity, the SM-3 IIB might be liquid fueled. The U.S. Navy generally avoids liquid-fueled missiles because they are difficult to manage on the open seas and more explosive and corrosive than solid fuel. According to a Navy official, however, "liquid-fuel is not a show stopper on ships," but would require additional precautionary measures and some engineering and equipment modifications in the launcher. Email communication from U.S. Navy official, June 2010; U.S. Navy, "Navy BMD Roles," PowerPoint presentation, June 15, 2010; interviews with naval analysts, June 2010.

36. Testimony of Lt. Gen. Patrick O'Reilly before the Senate Foreign Relations Committee, June 16, 2010.

37. Interview with Pentagon official, April 2010.

38. "Russia Will Not Accept Threat to Its Nuclear Deterrent—Lavrov," *Ria Novosti*, March 10, 2010.

39. Rogozin, "Missile Defence as a Common Cause for All," *Jane's Defence Weekly*, October 21, 2009.

40. Interviews with State Department officials, April and June 2010; Frank A. Rose, "Prospects for U.S.-Russia Missile Defense Cooperation," remarks at the Eleventh RUSI Missile Defence Conference, London, May 27, 2010.

41. Excerpts from Obama interview, *New York Times*, April 5, 2010, http://www.nytimes.com/2010/04/06/world/06armstext.html?ref=world.

42. Russian Federation, "The Military Doctrine of the Russian Federation," approved February 5, 2010; "Lavrov Stakes Out Treaty Limits," *Moscow Times*, April 7, 2010.

43. Interview with Pentagon officials, March and April 2010.

44. Testimony of Secretary of Defense Robert Gates before the Senate Armed Services Committee, June 17, 2010.

45. DOD, Fiscal Year (FY) 2011 Budget Estimates, *Research, Development, Test and Evaluation, Defense-Wide, Volume 3B*, Office of Secretary of Defense, February 2010, p. 257.

46. Elaine Grossman, "Cost to Test U.S. Global Strike Missile Could Reach $500 Million," *Global Security Newswire*, March 15, 2010; David Sanger and Thom Shanker, "U.S. Faces Choice on New Weapons for Fast Strikes," *New York Times*, April 23, 2010, p. A1.

47. Defense Advanced Research Projects Agency, *Justification Book Volume 1, Research, Development, Test and Evaluation, Defense-Wide—0440, Fiscal Year 2011 Budget Estimates*, February 2010, pp. 304–5 and 310–11. An April 2010 HTV test flight resulted in a fatal crash after nine minutes. Carlo Munoz, "DARPA, Air Force Assembling Joint Team to Review Failed CPGS Test," *Inside the Air Force*, May 7, 2010.

48. Testimony of Dr. James Miller before the Senate Foreign Relations Committee, June 16, 2010.

49. Vitaly Denisov, "Keepers of the Nuclear Stockpile," *Krasnaya Zvezda*, September 4, 2009.

50. Senate Armed Services Committee, "Advance Questions for General James E. Cartwright, USMC, Nominee for the Position of Vice Chairman of the Joint Chiefs of Staff," July 9, 2009.

51. Interviews with Pentagon officials, March and April 2010; National Research Council, *U.S. Conventional Prompt Global Strike: Issues for 2008 and Beyond* (Washington, DC: National Academies Press, 2008); Defense Science Board, *Time Critical Conventional Strike from Strategic Standoff* (March 2009), pp. 29–30; Bruce Sugden, "Speed Kills: Analyzing the Deployment of Conventional Ballistic Missiles," *International Security* summer 2009, pp. 141–44.

52. Interviews with Pentagon officials, March-June 2010; and Carlo Munoz, "DOD Still Grappling with Ambiguity Issues Tied to Prompt Global Strike," *Inside the Pentagon*, February 11, 2010.

53. White House, "Statements by President Obama and President Medvedev of Russia After Bilateral Meeting," Singapore, November 15, 2009.

54. Government Accountability Office, *Military Transformation: DOD Needs to Strengthen Implementation of Its Global Strike Concept and Provide a Comprehensive Investment Approach for Acquiring Needed Capabilities*, April 2008.

55. The analysis is being conducted by the Office of the Undersecretary of Defense for Acquisition, Technology, and Logistics to support the FY2012 budget request.

56. DOD, *Nuclear Posture Review Report*, p. 13.

About the Author

Micah Zenko is fellow for conflict prevention in the Center for Preventive Action at the Council on Foreign Relations. Previously, he worked at Harvard University's Kennedy School of Government and in Washington, DC, at the Brookings Institution, the Congressional Research Service, the Wisconsin Project on Nuclear Arms Control, and in the State Department's Office of Policy Planning. Zenko has published on a range of national security issues, including articles in the *Journal of Strategic Studies, Parameters, Defense and Security Analysis*, and *Annals of the American Academy of Political and Social Science* and op-eds in the *Washington Post, Los Angeles Times, Chicago Tribune*, and *Boston Globe*. He and Paul B. Stares coauthored a Council Special Report, *Enhancing U.S. Preventive Action*, which analyzes U.S. government capacity for different types of preventive action.

Zenko received a PhD in political science from Brandeis University. His book *Between Threats and War: U.S. Discrete Military Operations in the Post–Cold War World* examines U.S. uses of limited military force, assessing their effectiveness at achieving military and political objectives.

Advisory Committee for
Toward Deeper Reductions in U.S. and Russian Nuclear Weapons

Bruce Blair
World Security Institute

Barry Blechman
Henry L. Stimson Center

Linton F. Brooks

Charles D. Ferguson
Federation of American Scientists

Robert Gard

James M. Goldgeier, *ex officio*
Council on Foreign Relations

Thomas E. Graham
Kissinger Associates

Matthew Henry Kroenig
Georgetown University

Robert Legvold
Columbia University

Michael A. Levi, *ex officio*
Council on Foreign Relations

Kenneth Luongo
Partnership for Global Security

Franklin C. Miller
The Scowcroft Group

Steven K. Pifer
Brookings Institution

Pavel Podvig
Stanford University

Steven Sestanovich, *ex officio*
Council on Foreign Relations

Angela Stent
Georgetown University

Center for Preventive Action
Advisory Committee

Mission Statement of the Center for Preventive Action

The Center for Preventive Action (CPA) seeks to help prevent, defuse, or resolve deadly conflicts around the world and to expand the body of knowledge on conflict prevention. It does so by creating a forum in which representatives of governments, international organizations, nongovernmental organizations, corporations, and civil society can gather to develop operational and timely strategies for promoting peace in specific conflict situations. The center focuses on conflicts in countries or regions that affect U.S. interests, but may be otherwise overlooked; where prevention appears possible; and when the resources of the Council on Foreign Relations can make a difference. The center does this by

– Issuing Council Special Reports to evaluate and respond rapidly to developing conflict situations and formulate timely, concrete policy recommendations that the U.S. government, international community, and local actors can use to limit the potential for deadly violence.

– Engaging the U.S. government and news media in conflict prevention efforts. CPA staff members meet with administration officials and members of Congress to brief on CPA's findings and recommendations; facilitate contacts between U.S. officials and important local and external actors; and raise awareness among journalists of potential flashpoints around the globe.

– Building networks with international organizations and institutions to complement and leverage the Council's established influence in the U.S. policy arena and increase the impact of CPA's recommendations.

– Providing a source of expertise on conflict prevention to include research, case studies, and lessons learned from past conflicts that policymakers and private citizens can use to prevent or mitigate future deadly conflicts.

Council Special Reports

Published by the Council on Foreign Relations

Internet Governance in an Age of Cyber Insecurity
Robert K. Knake; CSR 56, September 2010
An International Institutions and Global Governance Program Report

From Rome to Kampala: The U.S. Approach to the 2010 International Criminal Court Review Conference
Vijay Padmanabhan; CSR No. 55, April 2010

Strengthening the Nuclear Nonproliferation Regime
Paul Lettow; CSR No. 54, April 2010
An International Institutions and Global Governance Program Report

The Russian Economic Crisis
Jeffrey Mankoff; CSR No. 53, April 2010

Somalia: A New Approach
Bronwyn E. Bruton; CSR No. 52, March 2010
A Center for Preventive Action Report

The Future of NATO
James M. Goldgeier; CSR No. 51, February 2010
An International Institutions and Global Governance Program Report

The United States in the New Asia
Evan A. Feigenbaum and Robert A. Manning; CSR No. 50, November 2009
An International Institutions and Global Governance Program Report

Intervention to Stop Genocide and Mass Atrocities: International Norms and U.S. Policy
Matthew C. Waxman; CSR No. 49, October 2009
An International Institutions and Global Governance Program Report

Enhancing U.S. Preventive Action
Paul B. Stares and Micah Zenko; CSR No. 48, October 2009
A Center for Preventive Action Report

The Canadian Oil Sands: Energy Security vs. Climate Change
Michael A. Levi; CSR No. 47, May 2009
A Maurice R. Greenberg Center for Geoeconomic Studies Report

The National Interest and the Law of the Sea
Scott G. Borgerson; CSR No. 46, May 2009

Planning for Post-Mugabe Zimbabwe
Michelle D. Gavin; CSR No. 31, October 2007
A Center for Preventive Action Report

The Case for Wage Insurance
Robert J. LaLonde; CSR No. 30, September 2007
A Maurice R. Greenberg Center for Geoeconomic Studies Report

Reform of the International Monetary Fund
Peter B. Kenen; CSR No. 29, May 2007
A Maurice R. Greenberg Center for Geoeconomic Studies Report

Nuclear Energy: Balancing Benefits and Risks
Charles D. Ferguson; CSR No. 28, April 2007

Nigeria: Elections and Continuing Challenges
Robert I. Rotberg; CSR No. 27, April 2007
A Center for Preventive Action Report

The Economic Logic of Illegal Immigration
Gordon H. Hanson; CSR No. 26, April 2007
A Maurice R. Greenberg Center for Geoeconomic Studies Report

The United States and the WTO Dispute Settlement System
Robert Z. Lawrence; CSR No. 25, March 2007
A Maurice R. Greenberg Center for Geoeconomic Studies Report

Bolivia on the Brink
Eduardo A. Gamarra; CSR No. 24, February 2007
A Center for Preventive Action Report

After the Surge: The Case for U.S. Military Disengagement from Iraq
Steven N. Simon; CSR No. 23, February 2007

Darfur and Beyond: What Is Needed to Prevent Mass Atrocities
Lee Feinstein; CSR No. 22, January 2007

Avoiding Conflict in the Horn of Africa: U.S. Policy Toward Ethiopia and Eritrea
Terrence Lyons; CSR No. 21, December 2006
A Center for Preventive Action Report

Living with Hugo: U.S. Policy Toward Hugo Chávez's Venezuela
Richard Lapper; CSR No. 20, November 2006
A Center for Preventive Action Report

Reforming U.S. Patent Policy: Getting the Incentives Right
Keith E. Maskus; CSR No. 19, November 2006
A Maurice R. Greenberg Center for Geoeconomic Studies Report

Foreign Investment and National Security: Getting the Balance Right
Alan P. Larson and David M. Marchick; CSR No. 18, July 2006
A Maurice R. Greenberg Center for Geoeconomic Studies Report

Challenges for a Postelection Mexico: Issues for U.S. Policy
Pamela K. Starr; CSR No. 17, June 2006 (Web-only release) and November 2006

U.S.-India Nuclear Cooperation: A Strategy for Moving Forward
Michael A. Levi and Charles D. Ferguson; CSR No. 16, June 2006

Generating Momentum for a New Era in U.S.-Turkey Relations
Steven A. Cook and Elizabeth Sherwood-Randall; CSR No. 15, June 2006

Peace in Papua: Widening a Window of Opportunity
Blair A. King; CSR No. 14, March 2006
A Center for Preventive Action Report

Neglected Defense: Mobilizing the Private Sector to Support Homeland Security
Stephen E. Flynn and Daniel B. Prieto; CSR No. 13, March 2006

Afghanistan's Uncertain Transition From Turmoil to Normalcy
Barnett R. Rubin; CSR No. 12, March 2006
A Center for Preventive Action Report

Preventing Catastrophic Nuclear Terrorism
Charles D. Ferguson; CSR No. 11, March 2006

Getting Serious About the Twin Deficits
Menzie D. Chinn; CSR No. 10, September 2005
A Maurice R. Greenberg Center for Geoeconomic Studies Report

Both Sides of the Aisle: A Call for Bipartisan Foreign Policy
Nancy E. Roman; CSR No. 9, September 2005

Forgotten Intervention? What the United States Needs to Do in the Western Balkans
Amelia Branczik and William L. Nash; CSR No. 8, June 2005
A Center for Preventive Action Report

A New Beginning: Strategies for a More Fruitful Dialogue with the Muslim World
Craig Charney and Nicole Yakatan; CSR No. 7, May 2005

Power-Sharing in Iraq
David L. Phillips; CSR No. 6, April 2005
A Center for Preventive Action Report

Giving Meaning to "Never Again": Seeking an Effective Response to the Crisis in Darfur and Beyond
Cheryl O. Igiri and Princeton N. Lyman; CSR No. 5, September 2004

Freedom, Prosperity, and Security: The G8 Partnership with Africa: Sea Island 2004 and Beyond
J. Brian Atwood, Robert S. Browne, and Princeton N. Lyman; CSR No. 4, May 2004

Addressing the HIV/AIDS Pandemic: A U.S. Global AIDS Strategy for the Long Term
Daniel M. Fox and Princeton N. Lyman; CSR No. 3, May 2004
Cosponsored with the Milbank Memorial Fund

Challenges for a Post-Election Philippines
Catharin E. Dalpino; CSR No. 2, May 2004
A Center for Preventive Action Report

Stability, Security, and Sovereignty in the Republic of Georgia
David L. Phillips; CSR No. 1, January 2004
A Center for Preventive Action Report

To purchase a printed copy, call the Brookings Institution Press: 800.537.5487.
Note: Council Special Reports are available for download from CFR's website, www.cfr.org.
For more information, email publications@cfr.org.